THE LITTLE GUIDE TO

KARL LAGERFELD

First published in 2025 by OH
An Imprint of HEADLINE PUBLISHING GROUP LIMITED

1

Disclaimer:

Cataloguing in Publication Data is available from the British Library

ISBN 978-1-03542-278-4

Compiled and written by: Katie Meegan
Editorial: Saneaah Muhammad
Designed and typeset in Avenir by: Stephen Cary
Project manager: Russell Porter
Production: Rachel Burgess
Printed and bound in Dubai

HEADLINE PUBLISHING GROUP LIMITED
An Hachette UK Company
Carmelite House, 50 Victoria Embankment, London EC4Y 0DZ

The authorised representative in the EEA is Hachette Ireland, 8 Castlecourt Centre,
Dublin 15, D15 XTP3, Ireland (email: info@hbgi.ie)

www.headline.co.uk   www.hachette.co.uk

THE LITTLE GUIDE TO

KARL LAGERFELD

STYLE TO LIVE BY

Unofficial and Unauthorized

CONTENTS

INTRODUCTION – 6

8

CHAPTER

ONE

BORN WITH PENCIL IN HAND

36

CHAPTER

TWO

AN AUTODIDACT IN PARIS

62

CHAPTER

THREE

LAGERFELD AND CHANEL

84

CHAPTER
FOUR

BRANCHING
OUT

106

CHAPTER
FIVE

ONWARDS AND
UPWARDS

142

CHAPTER
SIX

POWDERED WIGS
AND PAMPERED
CATS

INTRODUCTION

Karl Lagerfeld is one of the most memorable figures in fashion history, a rare case of a designer whose fame outshone any brand he represented. Lagerfeld's ascent to icon status was documented relentlessly throughout the 2000s, as photographs of him with the biggest names in celebrity became a mainstay in fashion magazines and tabloids alike. The pictures, taken at Chanel runway shows or glamorous celebrity events, were usually accompanied by a controversial quote or two from the ever-outspoken designer.

Lagerfeld, as he put it himself, was always impeccable. Right into his eighties, he retained the poise of a much younger man, consistently camera-ready with his powdered ponytail, starched white collar, black suit and glasses. His beloved cat, Choupette, often accompanied him for public appearances, becoming a celebrity in her own right, held close to his chest behind leather-gloved hands.

Hailing from Germany, a young Lagerfeld was naturally gifted in sketching, with a fascination for history that continued throughout his life. His journey began by chance in the early 1950s, after moving to Paris and gaining recognition by winning the first prize in a design competition. From this point, Lagerfeld paved a career ahead of its time in many ways, focusing on freelancing over commitment and ready-to-wear garments over made-to-measure fashion.

Perhaps the most fascinating thing about Lagerfeld was his outstanding work ethic. His razor-sharp focus and continued grasp of the zeitgeist were key factors in his unrivalled success. Lagerfeld entirely rejected nostalgia, prioritizing instead forward momentum and reinvention. He surrounded himself with young people and books, his indispensable sources of vitality and knowledge.

One need look no further than the dozens of glowing obituaries from celebrity friends and muses after his passing in 2019 to understand how Karl's enormous generosity and wit enriched the lives of many, and that his loss is still felt today.

CHAPTER
ONE

BORN WITH PENCIL IN HAND

KARL LAGERFELD (ORIGINALLY, LAGERFELDT) WAS BORN IN HAMBURG IN 1933 TO ELISABETH AND OTTO LAGERFELDT. HIS FATHER HAD MADE HIS FORTUNE THROUGH AN EVAPORATED MILK BUSINESS.

THE COUPLE, ALONG WITH KARL AND THEIR TWO DAUGHTERS, LEFT THE CITY FOR THE NEARBY TOWN OF BAD BRAMSTEDT AT THE OUTBREAK OF WORLD WAR TWO.

I felt loved and protected by
my parents – in a time like the 40s
when it was not easy to have a
protected life.

Karl Lagerfeld

Defending his parents and upbringing when he was accused of
sugarcoating it by the press, letter to Alicia Drake published on
wwd.com, September 12 2006

My mother and father were very well groomed. They always said that there is nothing worse than to be casually dressed when you are past the first flush of youth.

Karl Lagerfeld

On inheriting a passion for fashion at an early age, *The Karl Lagerfeld Diet*, Dr Jean-Claude Houdret, 2005

"

My parents weren't interested
[in my sisters]. They put them in
school and they married when they
came out. I could do what I wanted
but I was an easy child. They were
troublemakers.

"

Karl Lagerfeld

On being the favourite Lagerfeld child, vogue.co.uk,
November 4, 2015

I was six years old… I was sitting on my mother's desk in the country estate, in the big house – on her desk, where I was not supposed to sit and sketch – and I said to myself: 'You will become very famous.'

Karl Lagerfeld

On his ambition beginning at a very early age, following in his polyglot parents' footsteps and learning French from as young as six years old, thecut.com, December 9, 2018

Karl had a special bond with his mother Elisabeth, who encouraged his interests, bringing him along to a fashion show in Hamburg as a teenager.

She encouraged her son to hold himself to a high standard of presentation at all times.

Yes. She was strong, funny, mean and exactly what I needed.

Karl Lagerfeld

On his mother keeping his ego in check, thecut.com, December 9, 2018

When I was a child, my mother always told me that you could wake up in the middle of the night and be deathly sick, so you always have to be impeccable… I think everyone should go to bed like they have a date at the door.

Karl Lagerfeld

Taking his mother's lessons to heart and looking presentable even when sleeping, interviewmagazine.com, April 27, 2009

You know, as a child I was told by my mother, you must learn nothing. You always have to depend on people, because then you have to make an effort to have the money that they will do it for you.

Karl Lagerfeld

Recalling his mother's business advice, thecut.com, December 9, 2018

At that age I only had one idea:
To get out of there. And my mother
said: 'Hamburg is supposed to be
the gate to the world, but it is
only the gate!'

Karl Lagerfeld

Recalling how Elisabeth supported his ambitions to
leave Germany, system-magazine.com, November 19, 2024

It was not even a subject.
My mother said it was just like
your hair colour.

Karl Lagerfeld

On his mother accepting him being gay without hesitation,
thecut.com, December 9, 2018

Karl's first love was for art, and he drew inspiration from all the sources available to him as a youngster in the German countryside.

In school, he was introverted and was more interested in sketching and reading than spending time in the company of the other children.

I spent my childhood in the country and started reading even before going to school. There was nothing else in my life but sketching and reading.

Karl Lagerfeld

His disciplined approach to his work was evident from a young age, nytimes.com, October 12, 2015

Mostly I was looking at a lot of picture books at that time with historical costumes – no children's books. Illustrations or drawings of women from Van Dyck or Rococo illustrations.

Karl Lagerfeld

On some of his earliest muses, system-magazine.com, November 19, 2024

I have been a huge fan of Harry Kessler since my early youth because of my mother. Even the way I dress is in a way inspired by him. The eight volumes of his diaries are always near my bedside in my houses. Kessler represents for me, Germany at its best.

Karl Lagerfeld

On being inspired by Harry Kessler, the dandy, writer and arts patron, system-magazine.com, November 19, 2024

I hated the company of other children. I wanted to be a grown-up person, to be taken seriously. I hated the idea of childhood; I thought it was a moment of endless stupidity.

Karl Lagerfeld

On being a precocious boy, advanced beyond his years, newyorker.com, March 12, 2007

Despite his German upbringing, Lagerfeld had a tenuous connection to the country in years to come – because of the period of German history that he was born into.

During his working life, he would lie about his year of birth to dissociate himself from the Nazi party coming to power.

I don't have the notion of the feeling of 'home,' or 'Heimat,' as the Germans say. That doesn't exist for me. I bring myself with me wherever I go, so it's okay.

Karl Lagerfeld

His lack of sentimenta ity in later life extended toward his native Germany, too, interviewmagazine.com, April 27, 2009

I'm very drawn to Germany, but to a Germany that doesn't exist any longer, [that] died in 1933. If they became Nazis again in Germany, I'd throw my passport out of the window… My mother said Germany without Jewish people is like a dish with no salt.

Karl Lagerfeld

On his native country and its past, thecut.com, December 9, 2018

You know, 1933, even today, means the far right… It is a terrible date in Germany and in world history. So, he said that he changed it because he did not want his birth date connected with such an infamous year.

Gerhard Steidl

Book publisher, on his friend's confession, *Paradise Now: The Extraordinary Life of Karl Lagerfeld*, William Middleton, 2023

I'm German in my mind…
but from a Germany that doesn't
exist anymore.

Karl Lagerfeld

Letting his struggles with his national identity be known,
newyorker.com, March 12, 2007

With Germany facing an economic downturn, the Lagerfelds agreed to let their teenage son complete his secondary school education in Paris, where his father Otto had an office.

He enrolled in a school there to major in history and drawing.

I was born with a pencil in my hand and have been drawing all my life. I was always interested in paper and pencil, reading and learning languages – that was what I was interested in. I did not care about the rest.

Karl Lagerfeld

From a young age, Karl's determination to follow his passions was clear, system-magazine.com, November 19, 2024

It has been there my entire life.
I was not interested in anything
else but books, books, books and
drawing paper.

Karl Lagerfeld

Happy to let other parts of life pass him by while focusing on his
only passion, system-magazine.com, November 19, 2024

I spent my childhood thinking that I was born too late, that I had missed all this fabulous life before the war, the ocean liners, the *Orient Express.*

Karl Lagerfeld

Hoping to find a more glamorous environment in Paris, businessinsider.com, February 24, 2024

A fortune teller said to me when I was very young, 'Your story is a strange one. For you, it really starts when it stops for the others.'

Karl Lagerfeld

On being ready to put work first from a young age and do whatever it took to get ahead in his career, harpersbazaar.com, June 21, 2019

Yes, the discovery of silent movies… was much more important to me than discovering the talkies. To me they are images. Like illustrations.

Karl Lagerfeld

Being inspired by the silent movie icons of the day, nytimes.com, October 12, 2015

CHAPTER TWO

AN AUTODIDACT IN PARIS

LAGERFELD BEGAN MAKING WAVES IN PARIS, WINNING THE 1954 INTERNATIONAL WOOL SECRETARIAT'S WORLDWIDE COMPETITION WITH HIS DESIGN FOR A COAT.

THIS COMPETITION WAS KNOWN FOR DISCOVERING MAJOR TALENT WITHIN THE INDUSTRY, WITH FELLOW WINNERS INCLUDING YVES SAINT LAURENT THAT SAME YEAR, OPENING DOORS FOR LAGERFELD TO FURTHER HIS CAREER.

Yes, I won a worldwide competition that was organized by the International Wool Secretariat. There were about 200,000 competitors, and I won the first prize for a coat I designed.
The coat was reproduced by Balmain. I went for the fitting while I was still at school doing my Abitur.

Karl Lagerfeld

His success in the competition led to him leaving school and joining the fashion world within the Balmain fashion house team, system-magazine.com, November 19, 2024

Balmain, who was one of the judges, asked me if I wanted to work in his studio and my parents said, 'Yes, OK, but if it doesn't work, then you go back to school.' So I worked because I hate to be taught. I like to teach myself. And I'm pretty cultivated.

Karl Lagerfeld

With support from the Lagerfelds, a determined star was born, vogue.co.uk, November 4, 2015

I was still in school when I moved to Paris. But it didn't take me long to discover that the essential thing in life – I'm talking about the 50s – was to be well dressed.

Karl Lagerfeld

On quickly learning how to get ahead in his new environment, *The Karl Lagerfeld Diet*, Dr Jean-Claude Houdret, 2005

If you don't daydream your life
is a nightmare.

Karl Lagerfeld

Ever the dreamer, beginning to reap the rewards of his daydreams,
nytimes.com, October 12, 2015

Karl Lagerfeld spent over three years with Balmain, working tireless hours on sketches of dresses for buyers and clients.

Here he learned the ropes, and the inner workings of the Parisian atelier.

I learnt in the most boring way in the world — when I was at Balmain, we didn't have photocopiers, so we had to sketch every dress… One was obliged to work from the day after the collection for three weeks, until two in the morning, sketching everything… That's why in my sketches, you can see every technical detail.

Karl Lagerfeld

Displaying his tenacity, faced with a tough Balmain workload, harpersbazaar.com, June 21, 2019

I never went to fashion design school. I am totally self-taught, an autodidact.

Karl Lagerfeld

His lack of formal tra ning didn't hold him back within the fashion world, system-magazine.com, November 19, 2024

I've been lucky. I didn't finish school. I learned nothing. It is all improvisation. And yet I am not doing badly. Happiness is not something life owes you.

Karl Lagerfeld

On loving to learn by doing, nytimes.com, October 12, 2015

Next for Karl came the Patou years, where he was taught the "old" ways of 1920s dressmaking.

This expanded his skillset, as he learned about production and materials, while developing his drawing abilities further.

But frustration grew for Lagerfeld while working at this company, as he tired of made-to-measure couture and its processes.

I hate power. I hate the idea of it and the attitude that it presupposes. I don't want to embody a power that threatens others. For me that's the worst thing in the world. Things should happen naturally.

Karl Lagerfeld

On avoiding positions of authority that would set him apart from others, *The Karl Lagerfeld Diet*, Dr Jean-Claude Houdret, 2005

"

His death marks the end of the era of craftspeople who could do it all.

"

Anna Wintour

The legendary editor-in-chief, acknowledging Karl's versatility, vogue.com, February 22, 2019

I really learnt how to do clothes at Patou, for five years. The dressmakers from the 1920s were still working there, and they taught me everything.

Karl Lagerfeld

Grateful for the opportunity to hone his craft, harpersbazaar.com, June 21, 2019

Karl loved loose cannons.
He loved creative, passionate
people. He especially loved those
that didn't follow the rules. Not
surprisingly, because he was all
those things himself.

Milla Jovovich

Actress and model, on her affinity with Lagerfeld and his love for
rule-breakers, vogue.co.uk, February 23, 2019

[It] became very dowdy and very bourgeois and it was just not trendy.

Karl Lagerfeld

On made-to-measure couture, which he grew tired of making at Patou, newyorker.com, March 12, 2007

With an ambition of never being bound to one company again, Karl left Patou after five years, a career shift that would allow him total immersion in the creative design process, without the hassle of directly employing or managing staff.

He soon secured freelance work with Chloé and Fendi, where he could work on more modern, 1960s ready-to-wear collections.

I never mix them up in my mind. That is the secret of the story. First of all, I prefer not to analyze why or why not. I have the feeling that when I am doing Fendi I am another person to when I am doing Chanel or my own line. I have no personality. I have three.

Karl Lagerfeld

On adapting his personality to each brand and recognizing their individuality, vogue.co.uk, November 4, 2015

"

He branched out alone as perhaps
the world's most dazzling freelancer,
designing multiple labels with
electric energy.

"

Anna Wintour

On Lagerfeld's innovative approach to work and his impact on the
brands he worked with, vogue.com, February 22, 2019

I am a nice person and easy to work with. I understand the problems of the people I work with, and I don't have ego problems or take myself too seriously. I take the work seriously, but that's it.

Karl Lagerfeld

On being amiable and getting along with his coworkers, system-magazine.com, November 19, 2024

During this time, Lagerfeld's celebrity began to grow, as he formed a group of glamorous young people known to frequent the hottest spots in Paris.

This troupe included Andy Warhol, whose film *L'Amour* (1973) he starred in, and fellow dandy Jacques de Bascher, who has been referred to as the love of Lagerfeld's life.

You have to understand something: nobody works for me. They are always paid by someone else. Nobody is dependent on me. Apart from the staff in my house, no one.

Karl Lagerfeld

On retaining his status as equals with his coworkers across the many brands he worked with, system-magazine.com, November 19, 2024

Karl had a lot of imagination and fantasy in his mind but he would never have allowed himself any room for error. And Jacques brought him all of that freedom. He lived vicariously through Jacques.

Diane de Beauvau-Craon

Socialite and friend, on Lagerfeld and de Bascher's relationship, *Paradise Now: The Extraordinary Life of Karl Lagerfeld*, William Middleton, 2023

First of all, I'm better groomed. And, also, he pushed people. I never push people.

Karl Lagerfeld

Teasing Andy Warhol by comparing the artist to himself, newyorker.com, March 12, 2007

"

He recognized earlier than most
that ready-to-wear wasn't just
couture-lite but the vibrant
centre of the new, accomplished
woman's lifestyle.

"

Anna Wintour

On Lagerfeld's perceptiveness and ability to capture a
shifting culture, vogue.com, February 22, 2019

Ready-to-wear had become like a kind of fake couture… So I said, 'Let's do the real stuff.'

Karl Lagerfeld

Ready to begin a new chapter after Patou, recognizing the potential of ready-to-wear fashion, newyorker.com, March 12, 2007

CHAPTER THREE

LAGERFELD AND CHANEL

THE BRAND THAT LAGERFELD IS MOST OFTEN ASSOCIATED WITH IS CHANEL.

ITS FOUNDER, COCO CHANEL, DIED IN 1971, AND FOR THE FOLLOWING DECADE THE BRAND DWINDLED. IN 1982, LAGERFELD WAS APPOINTED ITS CREATIVE DIRECTOR, DESPITE THE WARNINGS OF HIS FRIENDS, WHO DIDN'T BELIEVE IN THE BRAND'S POTENTIAL FOR RESURGENCE.

BUT OF COURSE, THE BRAND CAME BACK TO LIFE.

When I started working at Chanel about 30 years ago, people told me not to touch it, it's dead, and it won't come back. But that's actually the main reason why I accepted – there is nothing better than a challenge.

Karl Lagerfeld

On rising to the challenge of revitalizing the brand, system-magazine.com, November 19, 2024

35 years ago, old labels were old labels. Now everybody wants to revive a label, and some of them, I don't think it's a good idea. But this was before Tom Ford and Gucci.

Karl Lagerfeld

His work with Chanel became the blueprint for rival brands' revivals, thecut.com, December 9, 2018

Karl's support transformed me from a shy German teenager into a supermodel. As intuitive as he was innovative, his advice, wit and inexhaustible energy were infectious and inspiring in equal measure. To his muse, he was my mentor, a profoundly cultured, kind and charismatic man.

Claudia Schiffer

Model, actor and Chanel catwalk regular in the 90's on Karl's effect on her personality and career, standard.co.uk, July 17, 2023

So to survive you have to cut the roots to make new roots. Because fashion is about today. You can take an idea from the past, but, if you do it the way it was, no one wants it.

Karl Lagerfeld

Defending his decisions when facxed with criticisms about how he modernized the Chanel brand, newyorker.com, March 12, 2007

Lagerfeld left his personal stamp upon the collections that followed during his reign as creative director.

Taking visual cues from popular 1980s streetwear, Chanel adopted its now signature embrace of maximalism, incorporating chains and logos galore.

Karl's role within the company extended into fashion photography, another string to his bow.

I do not have an ego trip. I don't care whether the brand that I'm working for is called Chanel or Fendi. What I do is the work, and the thing that matters is that I can do it under good conditions.

Karl Lagerfeld

A positive work environment is key for Lagerfeld, regardless of the brand, system-magazine.com, November 19, 2024

For the 1987 collections, the photographers were bad. Éric Pfrunder the image director shot the collection three times with different photographers, and it still was not very good. Then he told me, if it is that complicated, we should do it ourselves. I got an assistant and a camera and did them myself. And then it developed from there: editorials, advertisements and even museums.

Karl Lagerfeld

On how he became a photographer at Chanel, system-magazine.com, November 19, 2024

The idea is to take the most iconic jacket of the 20th century and make it in a way that couldn't have been made until the 21st.

Karl Lagerfeld

Modernizing the classic Chanel jacket, using the original Chanel pieces as a moodboard, vogue.co.uk, November 4, 2015

A collection is not just one basic idea. It comes from something that is in the air, something you suddenly like and put down on paper and then work out. People today are so used to taking one theme and staying with it all the way. I don't do that… I'm more interested in working out technical ideas than I am in themes or illustrating a scene or a country.

Karl Lagerfeld

On his collection inspirations, interviewmagazine.com, April 27, 2009

Lagerfeld found himself in the eye of the perfect storm. Chanel was perfectly placed to reap the benefits of the 1990s supermodel era, when fashion shows became bigger events than ever before.

As a result of their success, he negotiated a reported salary of $1 million from the brand, along with thousands worth of free items to gift his famous friends with.

> **"**
>
> Karl was a genius and always so kind and generous to me both personally and professionally. **"**

Victoria Beckham

After posing for a 2012 photoshoot with Lagerfeld in Paris, harpersbazaar.com, June 21, 2019

You cannot dance at three parties on the same evening. I always said to my investors to put it on another level and make it affordable. I think that's a modern attitude.

Karl Lagerfeld

Straddling the line between high and low culture with his work, theguardian,com, March 25, 2014

"

Some designers are very elitist, and, though Karl was a snob in some ways, he was also very democratic. He wanted to appeal to the world – I mean, he wanted everyone to come to his party.

"

Anna Wintour

On Karl's populist appeal, *Paradise Now: The Extraordinary Life of Karl Lagerfeld*, William Middleton, 2023

Luxury is to spend a lot on what you really don't need. But it's an industry and there's nothing bad about that. I prefer to make clothes than arms. Maybe you can be dressed to kill… but dresses, they don't kill anybody.

Karl Lagerfeld

On the meaning of luxury, vogue.co.uk, November 4, 2015

Karl's successes at Chanel gave him access to A-list celebrities. The top models of the 1980s, right through to the 2010s, all flocked to him.

Most of them have gushed to journalists about how much of a pleasure he was to work with.

It's not being perfect. What one needs is a face that people can identify in a second. That's why the girls who were famous in the 90s can still work for advertising. People know their faces.

Karl Lagerfeld

On the secret to being a timeless supermodel,
interviewmagazine.com, April 27, 2009

When Kendall was walking in his shows all the time, he would say to her, 'Please give this to your mother', and send me gifts. He was always so supportive of her, and he always remembered me. He was the kindest and most generous man.

Kris Jenner

Kardashian "momager" matriarch loved when her daughters worked with Karl, vogue.co.uk, February 23, 2019

"

Luxury is something very few people have… And to buy a handbag is to have a dream of getting nearer. That's our culture and tons of people – me included – make a lot of money from it.

"

Karl Lagerfeld

Discussing the psychological appeal of luxury brands, nytimes.com, October 12, 2015

"

The only thing more inspiring than Karl's vision, talent and creativity was his heart. He was one of the first designers I worked with in Paris, and that initial collaboration – and every time we worked together since – shaped my perspective of the fashion industry.

"

Karlie Kloss

American Chanel muse of the 2010s, on working with Karl, vogue.co.uk, February 23, 2019

Before, fashion was easy, in a way… There was the couture collection – people were inspired by that, they copied it, and that was the fashion in the world. Now fashion comes from the street, from other designers, from ready-to-wear, so high fashion has to be the fashion of the moment.

Karl Lagerfeld

Explaining why the 80s shift in Chanel's aesthetics was necessary, newyorker.com, March 12, 2007

CHAPTER
FOUR

BRANCHING OUT

THERE WAS NO SLOWING DOWN FOR KARL AS HE APPROACHED HIS SIXTIES. IN FACT, THE NEW MILLENNIUM ONLY SAW AN EXPANSION OF THE LAGERFELD EMPIRE.

LAGERFELD'S NEW ENDEAVOURS INCLUDED HIM PUBLISHING SEVERAL BOOKS (INCLUDING ONE ABOUT HIS DIET), OPENING BOOKSTORES, RELEASING A COMPILATION ALBUM OF HIS FAVOURITE TRACKS, AND A H&M COLLECTION IN 2004.

I have so much to do that all my
projects are related to my work.
I am not unhappy though. I don't
think of myself as an artist, and
I never have. I'd rather think of
myself as someone who does what
he needs to do, does what is
expected of him and concentrates
on the world he engages in.

Karl Lagerfeld

Humbly describing his attitude to his enormous workload,
system-magazine.com, November 19, 2024

If you think it's too many, you don't take those contracts. You know, I hate the designers who take the money and then go, [he gasps theatrically] 'It's too much!' For me, it's normal. But I'm not normal so I don't know. I like to do it. I don't have to force myself.

Karl Lagerfeld

The hectic fashion lifestyle suited Karl, although it wasn't for everyone, vogue.co.uk, November 4, 2015

I'm pretty good, but it bores me. Not the people, but the whole thing. What for? It's not very productive. I only want to do what I have to do: fashion, photography, books. And that's all.

Karl Lagerfeld

On nightlife, which he no longer cared for as he focused more on work, newyorker.com, March 12, 2007

I like to decorate, but I don't have time for anything. I sit in my atelier, where I draw and live and sleep. For guests I do have another building, because I want to be left alone. 99

Karl Lagerfeld

On designing his life around his work and having space to himself, system-magazine.com, November 19, 2024

With Chanel scheduling up to eight collections a year, Lagerfeld was working on up to seventeen collections in total across his several affiliated brands.

He managed to maintain this pace and consistency over 54 years of working, yet still somehow found time for extra commitments and countless media appearances.

I don't know how to cook, I don't know how to make a bed. I only know sketching and talking and making collections.

Karl Lagerfeld

Lagerfeld was self-deprecating about his abilities outside his talents in fashion, thecut.com, December 9, 2018

And I think I work better now than before. My brain is clearer.

Karl Lagerfeld

Feeling as though his focus sharpened as he aged, thecut.com, December 9, 2018

I am never happy. Happiness scares me; then I am afraid to be less happy. Happiness is a very dangerous state of mind.

Karl Lagerfeld

On understanding the double-edged sword of happiness, elle.com, February 20, 2019

When things are too positive and too sweet, it is very bad... Too peaceful is very dangerous. You fall asleep. You need to take care of your enemies. Your friends you don't need to worry about.

Karl Lagerfeld

Lagerfeld feared slowing down and experiencing the good all the time, understanding the need for balance, nytimes.com, October 12, 2015

Everything was possible. Anything that people have suggested to do, has been done – otherwise I would stop. I am not fighting windmills. I am not Don Quixote.

Karl Lagerfeld

When discussing his accomplishments, Lagerfeld humbly denied that he executed the impossible, system-magazine.com, November 19, 2024

At the heart of this, what some may define as workaholism, was a man determined to stay in the know, to remain up to date with the beating heart of culture.

An avid collector of books, he spoke in interviews about how he had amassed a massive collection.

My curiosity is just like antennas on roofs, you know? I want to know everything, I read all the newspapers – I want to keep up to date.

Karl Lagerfeld

On constantly striving to know more, system-magazine.com, November 19, 2024

Books were food for Karl.

Sébastien Jondeau

Karl's bodyguard and friend saw how important literature
was to the man, theguardian.com, April 15, 2023

Today the world comes to you. I read every magazine and everything. There are very few people as informed as I am.

Karl Lagerfeld

Even in his eighties, Karl was aware that his cultural knowledge rivalled his much younger contemporaries, thecut.com, December 9, 2018

I have assistants who inform me [about] what I have not seen. Personally, I have no time. I don't do internet, I don't do Facebook. I have to sketch, I have to play with Choupette, I have to sleep. The day is too short for that.

Karl Lagerfeld

Determined to say updated despite his aversion to the internet and his busy schedule, thecut.com, December 9, 2018

Despite his unrivalled productivity, and unstoppable ambition, Lagerfeld felt deeply frustrated with himself for a considerable duration of his career, always feeling as though he wasn't doing enough or that he was lazy.

I always have the feeling I could do better. I always feel I am behind a glass wall that I cannot break to get through to what I want.

Karl Lagerfeld

Lagerfeld felt like there was an invisible force which held him back from his full potential, nytimes.com, October 12, 2015

I always think I'm lazy, maybe
I could do better, I could make more
effort… But maybe when I get
through, then it's over.

Karl Lagerfeld

This invisible force also appeared to be motivating for Karl,
theguardian,com, March 25, 2014

I am always in a bad mood with myself, not with others. I'm never satisfied with myself. I'm always pushing myself. And normally, I do everything by myself. I do not have a studio with assistants who draw. If something is not done by me, I'm not interested.

Karl Lagerfeld

On the impact of his rigid self-discipline, system-magazine.com, November 19, 2024

I think I'm lazy and I could do more, and better. But, you know, I don't smoke, I don't drink, I have never taken drugs… I wouldn't say that I always watch other people but in a way I have always been apart. In the 60s and 70s, if you were not drinking and smoking and taking drugs, it was difficult.

Karl Lagerfeld

On how his focus often made him feel like an outsider, vogue.co.uk, November 4, 2015

CHAPTER
FIVE

ONWARDS AND UPWARDS

ONE OF LAGERFELD'S GREAT CONTRADICTIONS IS HOW HE WAS AN AVID COLLECTOR, WITH EXTENSIVE VOLUMES OF BOOKS AND POSTERS, AND YET AT THE SAME TIME A MAN WHO UTTERLY REJECTED NOSTALGIA, REFUSING THE NOTION THAT HE SHOULD AMASS POSSESSIONS OR ARCHIVAL MATERIAL OF HIS OWN.

> **"**
>
> I work for the rubbish bin. If someone wants a drawing, I have to do it. I love the process of drawing and making, but I am not interested in keeping something I've done.
>
> **"**

Karl Lagerfeld

Karl Lagerfeld threw out a lot of his design drafts and drawings, much to the chagrin of students and archivists, system-magazine.com, November 19, 2024

I try not to be sentimental and obsessive about possessions. I love collecting, but I hate owning.

Karl Lagerfeld

On rejecting the ownership of material possessions, elle.com, February 20, 2019

"

I always said, 'If it's over, it's over…'
If modelling is over, it's still the best
experience of my life. If it stops
tomorrow, I'll be friends with Karl
forever.

"

Brad Kroenig

On his bond with Lagerfeld that went much deeper than work,
nytimes.com, January 16, 2015

66

Nowadays, rich people wait for things to become expensive before they buy them. And why? Because they may not be flattered to have something in their house that they bought for little money, even if it is great. But you know, I had Warhols and Basquiats and I gave them away because I thought they would not last.

99

Karl Lagerfeld

Karl Lagerfeld rejected the notion that cost equates with value, nytimes.com, October 12, 2015

This rejection of sentimentality and nostalgia extended to Karl's professional life, too, as he refused to be retrospective, valuing his ability to remain in the present moment without distraction.

I am not like all those art directors now, who have 20 people sketching. I do it all myself. There's an old German dictum – 'no credit in the past.' And with those words I can manage.

Karl Lagerfeld

This German expression was something of a mantra to the designer, nytimes.com, October 12, 2015

"

I don't want to do anything over again, ever again. I want only to do what I haven't done. There's no 'again'. There's only the future. I hate the past – especially my own past.

"

Karl Lagerfeld

Rebirth and renewal were key components of Karl's creative process, interviewmagazine.com, April 27, 2009

Do you know what the beginning of the end is? Complacency.

Karl Lagerfeld

To Karl, stopping was equivalent to a death of sorts, system-magazine.com, November 19, 2024

I do not have a past. *Ich erinnere mich daran nicht.* I don't remember.

Karl Lagerfeld

Rejecting the past entirely was the only way Karl could progress by reminding himself, in German and in English, not to remember, system-magazine.com, November 19, 2024

For Lagerfeld fans, his major personal reinvention took place just as he reached the peak of his fame.

Karl had gained weight after Jacques de Bascher became sick with AIDS (and eventually passed away), only to lose it again and re-emerge with the iconic new look he is most associated with.

The imagination can transform all sorts of personal insanity into elements of self-invention, and you need to make use of this.

Karl Lagerfeld

Karl fuelled his desire for reinvention into his weight-loss programme, detailed in his diet book, The Karl Lagerfeld Diet, Dr Jean-Claude Houdret, 2005

Ever looking forward, without nostalgia, Karl was scared of nothing. Carried by an exceptional capacity to reinvent himself, he excelled in every domain.

Babeth Djian

Friend and journalist, on Lagerfeld's chameleon-like ability, numero.com, September 3, 2020

I have one instinct stronger than any other thing in life, and that is the instinct for survival.

Karl Lagerfeld

Karl's desire to remain alive triumphed over all adversaries, newyorker.com, March 12, 2007

> "
> Karl was the living soul of fashion: restless, forward-looking, and voraciously attentive to our changing culture.
> "

Anna Wintour

Friend and fashion editor, on how Karl's proclivity for reinvention reflected the nature of fashion itself, vogue.com, February 22, 2019

Lagerfeld's tendency to reinvent himself and reject nostalgia also had its downsides.

It impacted upon the people around him, who never knew when the fiery designer might drop them entirely.

He had several high-profile personal feuds, including ones with fellow designer and former friend Yves Saint Laurent and former muse Claudia Schiffer.

I have an entourage of people of today. Because people can work with me for a hundred years but they have to stay informed. And no regrets, no remove, not saying, 'Oh, things were better then.'

Karl Lagerfeld

On ensuring that the people he was surrounded with remained informed, newyorker.com, March 12, 2007

> "
>
> He switched people out because he always had to be moving. He always knew exactly what he wanted... I already knew that it would end at some point... I had already seen him cut ties with plenty of people, like Inès de la Fressange, Claudia Schiffer, Céline Toledano and Gilles Dufour at Chanel.
>
> "

Eric Wright

Fendi coworker, on parting ways with Lagerfeld, which he knew would enc their friendship, *Karl Lagerfeld: A Life in Fashion*, Alfons Kaiser, 2022

It's too easy to forgive. I love revenge. Forgiving is not my favourite thing. I can forget by indifference, but not forgive.

Karl Lagerfeld

Karl lived passionately, headstrong and set in his ways, elle.com, February 20, 2019

> **"**
>
> He would burn his bridges… He could be like the little spoiled boy back in Germany, who has had everything he ever wanted. He would have a temper tantrum and just get rid of people. If you do things with Karl, you know the rules and you have to make sure you don't break them.
>
> **"**

André Leon Talley

The American fashion journalist recounts Lagerfeld's fickle side, *Paradise Now: The Extraordinary Life of Karl Lagerfeld*, William Middleton, 2023

I like my friends to have their own life. I want nobody to depend on me. I love children, but other people's children.

Karl Lagerfeld

Karl enjoyed his independence, without the worry of having others rely on him, thecut.com, December 9, 2018

Karl found himself surrounded by much younger friends in his old age, as he loved forming bonds with talented young people who were independent and who inspired him – much like himself.

I have friends from a younger generation. My generation all talk about their health and I don't want that.

Karl Lagerfeld

Karl found friends whose interests aligned with his, vogue.co.uk, November 4, 2015

"

So many people are afraid of him, and that's the worst thing… It shuts the door immediately. What he likes is that one be engaged in conversation – and more than anything, that one be informed.

"

Amanda Harlech

On Lagerfeld's taste in friends, wmagazine.com, February 19, 2019

I'm surrounded by young people, but I am not a lesson-giver. I had a lot of people, not all of them were successful, but most of the people I work with here, they've never worked for somebody else.

Karl Lagerfeld

Karl never saw himself as a mentor to his young friends and collaborators, instead putting himself on the same level as the next generation, thecut.com, December 9, 2018

Two of Karl's most significant relationships in his later years were with young male models Brad Kroenig and Baptiste Giabiconi.

He would appear alongside them at public appearances, facing rumours that he was romantically involved. However, Lagerfeld insisted these men were like family to him, with Kroenig even making Karl the godfather of his child.

I see them like family. I have no family at all, so it's good to have, like, sons, but without the unpleasant problems sons can create.

Karl Lagerfeld

Karl believed he had found the security that family can provide without the downsides, nytimes.com, January 16, 2015

I don't have children myself but
I am very well with other people's,
like my famous godson.

Karl Lagerfeld

Hudson Kroenig, Karl's godson, would often model children's
collections on the runway at Chanel shows, vogue.co.uk,
November 4, 2015

"

Karl is fascinated by being so close to a young mind… It's very new for Karl.

"

Amanda Harlech

British creative consultant and writer, on Lagerfeld's godfatherly duties, nytimes.com, January 16, 2015

My job is not to dwell on my past in complacency.

Karl Lagerfeld

Karl saw items from the past as something that would hold him back creatively, system-magazine.com, November 19, 2024

Despite Karl's disavowal of the past and refusal to ruminate in it, he retained a fascination with history that was evident throughout his boyhood.

Some things in the past, he did admit, were better. Lagerfeld tended to contact collaborators by fax, long after the practice became antiquated.

"

He was the original multitasker,
a man who did everything
at once.

"

Anna Wintour

On Karl's ability to do it all, wwd.com, June 20, 2019

I love using a fax all the time, every day. With all the buttons, I feel like a bad secretary! Do you know what is most irritating? It's when a computer auto-corrects! You can't play with words anymore. It makes me hysterical.

Karl Lagerfeld

Karl felt that computers were a less creative means for communication, system-magazine.com, November 19, 2024

I'm not sure how he was able to get dressed in an outfit like this every day.

Tommy Hilfiger

The iconic fashion designer wore a suit reminiscent of Lagerfeld's trademark look to the 2023 Met Gala hosted in memory of the designer, cnn.com, May 2, 2023

I hate selfies… Don't use your film for ugly purpose.

Karl Lagerfeld

Selfies were another modern innovation that didn't receive the Lagerfeld seal of approval, nytimes.com, January 16, 2015

CHAPTER
SIX

POWDERED WIGS
AND
PAMPERED CATS

KARL LAGERFELD FAILED TO
SHOW UP FOR THE CLOSING OF
A 2019 CHANEL COUTURE SHOW
IN PARIS, RAISING SPECULATION
REGARDING HIS WELL-BEING.

HE DIED AGED 85, ON
FEBRUARY 19, 2019, AT THE
AMERICAN HOSPITAL IN PARIS,
DUE TO COMPLICATIONS RELATED
TO PANCREATIC CANCER.

"

He fine honed the art of laughing everything off, and would always have a kind word for anyone who approached him. I have always admired his extreme modesty, his immense freedom of spirit and emotional intelligence.

"

Babeth Djian

Magazine editor and Karl's friend, on their special bond, numero.com, September 3, 2020

One day it will be over and I don't care. As my mother used to say, 'There is one God for everybody and all religions are shops.'

Karl Lagerfeld

Karl appeared comfortable with his own mortality, and shared his views on spirituality, nytimes.com, October 12, 2015

66

Karl is really generous… He likes his friends to look chic.

99

Brad Koenig

On Lagerfeld's tendency to shower his closest friends in expensive gifts, *The New York Times* magazine, January 16, 2015

I think the people around me
I can really trust. Even the
people in my house. My maids.
Or Choupette's.

Karl Lagerfeld

On being surrounded by trusted accomplices in the later stages
of his career, vogue.co.uk, November 4, 2015

In his later years, Lagerfeld spoke about embracing old age.

Although the designer didn't grow old with any significant partner, he refuted the notion that this made him lonely.

This is another cliché – the *loneliness*. I have to fight to be alone! And you have to recharge the batteries. People who can't be alone have a problem. Loneliness is a luxury for people like me.

Karl Lagerfeld

On the luxury of loneliness, newyorker.com, March 12, 2007

Through decades of adventures and misadventures, he was a true and loyal friend.

Anna Wintour

Paying tribute to her good friend after his passing, vogue.com, February 22, 2019

If you are sick and old with no money then it must be hard, but in my case it is the height of luxury to be alone.

Karl Lagerfeld

Karl felt that the privileges of wealth shielded him from any hardship in old age, vogue.co.uk, November 4, 2015

However, there was one later-in-life Lagerfeld relationship that stood out as more important than the rest. His cat Choupette became something of a life partner to him from 2011 onwards.

In interviews, he sometimes shared his feeling that she may be his mother reincarnated in cat form.

Everything is controlled by her. She wakes me up at 7am because she wants me to bring her fresh croquettes, she won't touch food from the night before, she gets offers for food commercials but it is out of the question. She is a kept woman.

Karl Lagerfeld

Karl's life began to revolve around his beloved cat, theguardian,com, March 25, 2014

> **"**
>
> He was so extreme in every single thing he did ... So, if he's going to have a cat, he's going to have a cat that has a diamond necklace. That cat had a better life than about 90% of the human beings on planet earth.
>
> **"**

Fran Lebowitz

American author, on Choupette's glamorous existence,
Paradise Now: The Extraordinary Life of Karl Lagerfeld,
William Middleton, 2023

I think Choupette made me a better person – less selfish... In one trashy French paper they asked the reader, 'Are you shocked that a cat can make so much money?' Eighty-two percent were shocked, so I sent the editor a letter saying I was sorry to find that 82 percent of their readers were envious people.

Karl Lagerfeld

On Choupette becoming a controversial success in her own right, nytimes.com, October 12, 2015

She's like a sentimental person. She's very funny – when I'm reading a newspaper, she reads it with me. She eats on the table, too, not on the floor. If the food is on the floor, she won't touch it. She's very human… I sometimes think she's my mother's reincarnation.

Karl Lagerfeld

On life at home with his feline companion, harpersbazaar.com, June 21, 2019

> He's one of the truest examples of being able to come to a country, and embody it. Sometimes it's very difficult to be a French designer if you're French, because you don't see the irony in something. You don't see the baguette, whereas Karl saw the baguette.

Jonathan Anderson

The creative director spoke at the memorial about Lagerfeld's French integration, wwd.com, June 20, 2019

In June 2019, a memorial service was held at the Grand Palais in Paris, titled "Karl For Ever".

Huge portraits of Lagerfeld adorned the walls of the historic building at this lavish event, attended by over 2,000 people, including some of the biggest names in fashion, politics and French high society.

There comes a moment in life when the idea of youth and beauty has to give way to style and elegance. That's how it is.

Karl Lagerfeld

Lagerfeld knew that the promises of youth had to be foregone to make way for glamour later in life, *The Karl Lagerfeld Diet*, Dr Jean-Claude Houdret, 2005

I imagine that Karl would have hated it! He would have come and said, 'What is this cathedral? How dreadful… There are some pictures that he wouldn't have liked so much because he was not thin, or something.

Inès de la Fressange

Designer and collaborator, on Karl's assumed response to such a memorial event would have been, wwd.com, June 20, 2019

160

I don't want to be on the internet.
I hardly use a credit card –
everything where you can be fixed.
I'm floating. Nobody can catch
me, mmm?

Karl Lagerfeld

Karl's desire for freedom and independence merged with his
dismissal of new technologies, newyorker.com, March 12, 2007

"

When I went to Chloé, he came out with an amazing statement that I just think is the coolest thing ever: he said, 'I knew they would take a big name to replace me at Chloé, but I thought it would be in fashion and not in music.' So chapeau to you, Karl!

"

Stella McCartney

The fashion designer and daughter of Paul McCartney, shared this funny anecdote at the event, wwd.com, June 20, 2019

Some of the musicians from the 60s, because there has been nothing better than them since, you know? What I like about music is the songs you can remember the lines of in a single second. The Beatles, The Rolling Stones.

Karl Lagerfeld

On his favourite musicians, all from an earlier era, interviewmagazine.com, April 27, 2009

163

The memorialization of Karl Lagerfeld didn't end there, however, with "Karl Lagerfeld: A Line of Beauty" selected as the theme for the 2023 Costume Institute Benefit (also known as the Met Gala).

Celebrities showed up for the annual event dressed in the designer's archival creations, paying homage to the man himself, or, in a few cases, donning full Choupette cosplay.

I thought, 'What is more Karl?'
You know, the iconic Chanel
pearls is what I always thought of.
So we wanted to just be dripping
in pearls.

Kim Kardashian

On wearing a dress inspired by Lagerfeld's maximalist
Chanel designs, cnn.com by CNN staff, May 2, 2023

The drawings are in honour of how Karl sketched. Honestly, this has been a wonderful process. But it's probably the most I've ever thought about an outfit.

Roger Federer

The Swiss former tennis champion, on his suit jacket with sketches on the inside, cnn.com by CNN staff, May 2, 2023

I fight against possessions. They victimize you… if not, little worthless things I would not mention.

Karl Lagerfeld

On staying free of material possessions, anothermag.com, June 21, 2019

Karl's legacy was further immortalized by a new television series. *Becoming Karl Lagerfeld* was released on Disney+ in the summer of 2024.

It focused upon Karl's feelings of being a German outsider in Paris, his career milestones at Chloé and Fendi, and his relationships with Jacques de Bascher and Yves Saint Laurent.

It gave me a freedom to create something personal, to surprise people with a more human, approachable, vulnerable, insecure Karl Lagerfeld.

Daniel Brühl

Lead actor in *Becoming Karl Lagerfeld*, on his depiction of the style icon, wmgazine.com, June 24, 2024

It's not a biopic in the classic sense. I think biopics tend to be a little inert. Here, on the contrary, what we're trying to convey is rather the soul, the motivations and the influences that were driving Karl Lagerfeld during this period in order to understand him better, quite simply.

Pascaline Chavanne

The costume designer, on the intent of the TV show, wwd.com, June 7, 2024

I'm not a very sociable person. I'm very at ease and good at small talk, but I don't have much time. And social life bores me. People don't bore me, social life bores me. But I'm perfectly happy.

Karl Lagerfeld

On comforts and happiness, anothermag.com, June 21, 2019

66

It's only when I focused on the 70s, that I found a story which isn't just opportunistic, about a famous person doing famous things, but is a real human drama… I felt, this is so rich, so universal, it will be something for everyone, including people who are not interested in Lagerfeld nor fashion.

Isaure Pisani Ferry

The screenwriter, on the show's appeal, thehollywoodreporter.com, June 13, 2024

Karl Lagerfeld left behind a fortune that is estimated to around $300 million dollars.

However, the rumoured inheritors of this fortune have been awaiting an outcome since his death.

Among them are Sébastien Jondeau, Baptiste Giabiconi, Brad and Hudson Koenig and, of course, Choupette's maid.

If people live only one life with not a very fun youth, they are frustrated. I did what I wanted whenever I wanted. It was pleasant, but today, I would be bored to death by it. If you want to look old, try to be young. Nothing is worse than that.

99

Karl Lagerfeld

Looking back fondly on his youth, on thecut.com, December 9, 2018

The adoption plan, which both seemed to have wanted, was odd, not least because Baptiste already has a father. But he did tell us that he loved Lagerfeld. In the end, a picture of Lagerfeld's almost monkish existence emerges.

Michael Waldman

BBC documentary maker, on Lagerfeld's plans to adopt model Baptiste Giabiconi, which ultimately fell through, theguardian.com, April 15, 2023

Virginie Viard, a longtime collaborator and friend of Lagerfeld's, took over his role at Chanel after his passing. The pair often closed out runway shows together.

She had worked at the company since 1987 and was regularly referred to as "Karl's right-hand woman".

But I know that I need other people… I take care of myself because broken cars are not that comfortable.

Karl Lagerfeld

Despite his introverted tendencies, Lagerfeld realized that he couldn't be entirely independent, nytimes.com, October 12, 2015

Yes, I never drink alcohol. I do not eat sugar or meat either.

Karl Lagerfeld

Lagerfeld's "will to survive" showed in his aspirations of superb health, system-magazine.com, November 19, 2024

As soon as I receive his sketches, the process begins. I try to please him, but I like to surprise him too.

Virginie Viard

On her and Karl's creative collaborative process, telegraph.co.uk, February 20, 2019

Our relationship is fundamental –
one of profound affection and a
true friendship.

Karl Lagerfeld

On the depth of his and Viard's relationship, telegraph.co.uk,
February 20, 2019

I saw then that I was among those who mattered to him.

Virginie Viard

On being asked to accompany Karl to Jacques de Bascher's funeral, wmagazine.com, February 19, 2019

Virgine Viard stepped down as creative director of Chanel in the summer of 2024, and fashion journalists have been speculating as to who will replace her ever since.

One thing is for certain: nobody will regain the pop culture chokehold of runway shows quite like Karl.

The last thing I want to be is a serious person. I can be serious but I don't want to show it. It's like being politically correct. Maybe I'm politically correct but don't make a subject out of it. It kills advanced conversation.

Karl Lagerfeld

On duality, anothermag.com, June 21, 2019

"

I am very flattered that Karl Lagerfeld draws inspiration from space for his collections... Thankfully he did not draw inspiration from astronauts' outfits.

"

Thomas Pesquet

French astronaut, who inspired the 2017 Chanel runway show, which featured a life-size model spaceship, wwd.com, May 6, 2017

Why a supermarket?
It is something of today's life and
even people who dress at Chanel
go there – it's a modern statement
for expensive things.

Karl Lagerfeld

Karl turned the Paris Grand Palais into a supermarket for
a 2014 runway show, Chanel branded goods and supermarket
trollies included, theguardian.com, March 4, 2014

Have you felt any warming this winter… Maybe that's all nonsense, who knows.

Karl Lagerfeld

Lagerfeld, ever the provocateur, erected a huge iceberg in the middle of the glass-domed Grand Palais and dressed models in fake fur in 2010, reuters.com, March 9, 2010

We wanted to set sail, to take
you on an actual cruise.

Bruno Pavlovsky

Karl's Chanel coworker explains the 148-metre-long ship
erected for their 2018 show, theguardian.com, May 4, 2018

Although it may feel as though the fashion world's creative heart remains missing, there may be more Lagerfeld surprises to come.

With news emerging in 2021 that Karl's photographic legacy was uploaded to the blockchain, here's to hoping he can continue to posthumously push fashion in exciting new directions.

This is a remarkable first step into the future as we pave our way into the virtual world of NFTs and digital fashion.

Pier Paolo Righi

CEO of the Lagerfeld brand, on launching an NFT collectible in the form of a digital Karl figurine, fashionunited.uk, September 10, 2021

I personally have nothing to say, nothing to explain. I make such big efforts to forget things. Non, non, non, I couldn't tell the truth.

Karl Lagerfeld

On living in the moment, anothermag.com, June 21, 2019

Beyond a fashion designer, Karl was a contemporary icon, and our night time shoots would generate real crowds in the streets of the capital: he was a veritable rock star.

Babeth Djian

Magazine editor, on her friend's star power, numero.com, September 3, 2020

191

You can only really build something new if you destroy the old.

Karl Lagerfeld

Immortal last words from the designer who will never be forgotten, anothermag.com, June 21, 2019

not even your

MOMMA
'N THEM

were

PIDDLIN'
ABOUT.

The stockin's were hung
by the chimney with care,

In hopes that St. Nicholas
pert near would be there.

The children were nestled
all snug in their pallet,

Dreamin' of divinity and strawberry pretzel salad.

And Mom in her kaftan

and me in my toboggan,

Had just taken to the bed to rest our

LIL' NOGGINS

When out on the roof,

There arose such a ruckus,

I sprang from my bed to see what nonsense was among us.

The moon looked real pretty—

*kinda made me
wish we had snow,*

But then I remembered
that'd be an emergency

*'cause we live in
the South, ya know?*

I near 'bout

CAUGHT THE VAPORS

'cause right there,

*Appeared a miniature sleigh
and eight tiny reindeer.*

*With a lil' ole bitty driver
so lively and quick,*

*I knew right then and there;
this must be St. Nick.*

Quick as

ALL GET~OUT,

those reindeer
they came,

*He whistled and called
every one of 'em by name.*

He said, "Now Dasher,
now Dancer,
now Prancer and Vixen,"

*"On Comet, on Cupid,
on Donner and Blitzen."*

And then,

I SWANNY,

I heard on the roof,

*The prancin' and pawin'
of each little hoof.*

I was clutchin' my

PEARLS

and was fixin' to
turn around,

*When down the chimney
came St. Nicholas with a bound.*

He didn't say nothin'
but he got right to work,

And he filled all them stockin's
and turned around with a jerk.

He smiled and said,
"Tell your momma
'n them I said,
'How are they doin'?'"

*"Let me let y'all go—
'cause I gotta get movin'."*

Very nimbly,
he went back up the chimney,

Got right back in that sleigh
and he gave 'em a whistle,

And away they all flew, and I knew I'd seen somethin' special.

But I heard him hollerin'
right before he got outta sight,

He said,
"MERRY
CHRISTMAS
to all y'all,
And to all y'all
a good night."

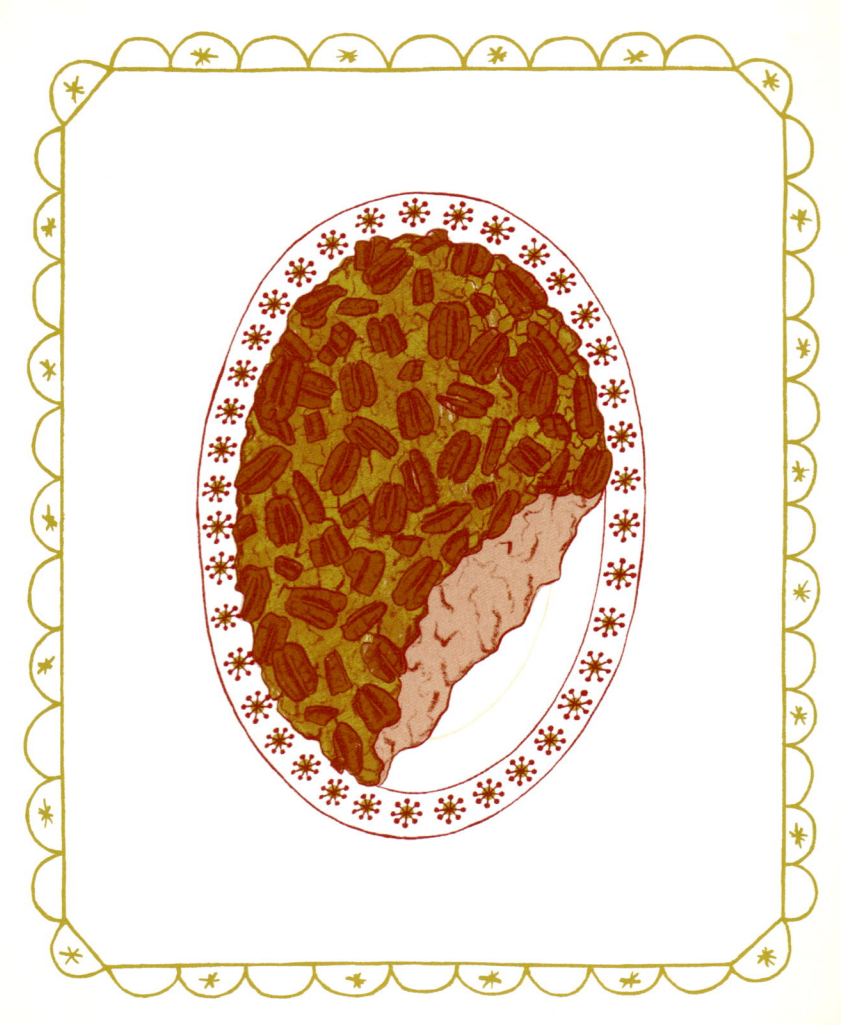

LANDON'S CHRISTMAS SWEET POTATO CASSEROLE

Sweet potato casserole—it can look like pumpkin pie, but it's not, y'all. In fact, I prefer it to pumpkin pie even though they're similar, and I'm not ashamed to admit it. A sweet potato casserole is one of my favorite desserts to eat on Christmas, and I hope you'll enjoy making it as much as you do eating it.

Casserole:

3 cups sweet potatoes,
  cooked and mashed
1 cup granulated sugar
½ cup butter or oleo,
  at room temperature
½ cup whole milk
1 tablespoon vanilla extract
2 eggs, beaten well
Pinch of cinnamon, if desired

Topping:

1 cup light brown sugar
½ cup butter or oleo,
  melted
½ cup all-purpose flour
1 cup chopped nuts

✳ Combine the ingredients for the casserole
  and mix well.

✳ Pour in a two-quart casserole dish.

✳ Combine topping ingredients and sprinkle
  on top of the casserole.

✳ Bake at 350°F for 30 to 35 minutes.

GLOSSARY
(in order of appearance)

✳ ✳ ✳ ✳ ✳✳

Momma 'n them: Your momma and anyone your momma is associated with.

Piddlin' about: Doing something that's not particularly important or useful.

Pert near: Almost.

Pallet: A bed on the floor that usually consists of a fitted sheet, cover, and sometimes an egg crate mattress topper.

Divinity: A fluffy Southern dessert made from egg whites, sugar, and corn syrup.

Strawberry pretzel salad: A salad made with pretzels, strawberries, and cream cheese. It does *not* have lettuce or greens.

Kaftan: A shapeless dress that can be made from different fabrics, and a step up from a housecoat. Not to be confused with a duster or a robe.

Toboggan: A winter hat. Not a mode of transportation in the winter.

Noggin: A person's head.

Ruckus: A disturbance or commotion.

Caught the vapors: Feeling faint, weak, or discomfort.

All get-out: Quick to the extreme.

I swanny: I swear.

Clutchin' my pearls: An amused exasperation or a state of shock.

Fixin' to: You're preparing or about to do something.

Let me let y'all go: A considerate way to give someone permission to leave.

Y'all: Refers to more than one person, and it is spelled Y-'-A-L-L, *not* Y-A-'-L-L.